Love and Savagery

Love and Savagery

Des Walsh

Talonbooks

Copyright © 2009 Des Walsh

Talonbooks
PO 2076, Vancouver, British Columbia, Canada V6B 3S3
www.talonbooks.com

Typeset in Tribute and printed and bound in Canada.
First printing, 2nd edition: 2009

The publisher gratefully acknowledges the financial support of the Canada
Council for the Arts; the Government of Canada through the Book Publishing
Industry Development Program; and the Province of British Columbia through
the British Columbia Arts Council and the Book Publishing Tax Credit for our
publishing activities.

Love and Savagery was first published by Talonbooks in 1989.

LIBRARY AND ARCHIVES CANADA CATALOGUING IN PUBLICATION

Walsh, Des
     Love and savagery / Des Walsh. — 2nd ed.

Poems.
ISBN 978-0-88922-599-2

     I. Title.
PS8595.A586L6 2009   811'.54   C2009-902119-6

For Brendan and Monica

On the city's steps

He saw the sun move around her
and wanted to say, I see flesh tones.
His hand gripped the cold steel rail,
sent his fingers trembling, back to his face
where he felt for some trace of her.
He looked for an historical mention,
some reference to her blinding light,
her effect on an empire.
He heard that wounded men would cry out
at the mere whisper of her name.

So it has started, his seed planted.
Back where the wind touches dry stone and water
he wanders endlessly in efforts to comfort her.
The marriage of canvas, language and brush stroke.
All there, on moulded steps, in the city,
where he would love her
and let the world have
exactly what it needed.

If she were blinded
by rebellious light
who would fix her hair
and place entries
in her diary.
Who would be dutiful
and abandon whatever
made them comfortable
only to read to her
and smooth her reluctant hands.

He needed to imagine her helpless,
without her sought after judicial strength.
Only then would he be sure of his place.
His voice would become a religion
and she would reunite her mythology
by leaning closer to his breast,
leaning closer to his heroic hunger.

He pleads with her,
listen closely
these hearts that open and close so carefully
are not meant for loving exercise.
They fit so few of us.

July 26, 1986

Yesterday, a southerly wind
harnessed every leaf in St. John's
moving the streets in beautiful,
turbulent disarray.
Boats, unlike leaves,
were tied securely to the waterfront,
a coastline of steel and tradition.
History tells us that on July 25, 1960,
the winds were calm and perfectly placed,
mothers kissed their children's future
and exotic birds were seen hovering
above the city's celebrations.
History will not repeat itself.

Don't leave me she said,
from somewhere underneath herself,
I'm afraid of what I might do.
And he didn't, aware of who she was
in some other life, the interpreter
of an oral race obsessed
with religion and witchcraft,
the mistress of late-night ritual
with soda crackers and tea ....
It's back to the dream for us he said,
back to the rolling surf and immoral chatter,
the possible rendezvous of former self
where screaming sea birds dip and plunge,
reeling toward the tumultuous shoreline
and their salt soggy weed bed,
knowing they had lied
and had no intention of feeding them
or any other.

It is light blue, the snow.
Making no mistake about where
it wants to be, it cloaks everything.
The birds are quiet about it, knowing
soon they will have the trees for protection.
Even exposed lovers are proving restless,
they brave February winds to hold each other.

Knowing this, and the risk of looking
in her eyes once more,
he paces St. John's,
blue light burns his face
as he sculptures her image on the Southside Hill.
Ships' whistles sound to acknowledge her,
pedestrians shuffle in mute salute.

He will weep no more
for the lost and broken hearted
in there mildewed tear-stained rooms,
happy to see him go.

Please read this, it's not a threat

Listen up, he says, this is what she wrote:
    "What's happening and where are you and why
    didn't you call me this morning? I need to
    talk to you. I need to hear your voice. I'm
    beginning to need you. I feel addicted."
Tasting this, he went about his business.

Later, the fly had completed its laps of the room
and he was almost ready to accept its routine,
he wanted to join the search for the open window.
All of the sweetness had left him nauseous
and he was almost ready to ignore her,
he wanted her damaged and lonely.

He was seen today.
The sun was warm,
he was eating fruit.

Complicated jewel of the Burin Peninsula,
why did you leave him wet and cold,
no trumpets for the parade
no announcement from the window.

Did you hear his heart on the doorstep
and ignore it only to protect the revolution,
choosing instead to let the rain wash
his love for you into the street.

There's nothing to give, nothing comes in return.
The green spruce is attaching itself to the city's edge.
All boundaries have been marked.

The kitchen, 127 Gower Street, St. John's, February 21, 1985

At the time of this writing
he is thirty years old.
An emotional legend,
he wanders between moments
and studies the brutal exchange
of night and day.
He fights with the habit of one plant
that struggles with its freedom,
pressing its veined green life
to the kitchen window.
The hot water boiler leak
continues its journey across the floor
with no sense of direction or style.
Will there be a purpose for the water,
life for the ivy ....
Why would she have turned around
and with her crow black eyes
cripple an already wounded child?
These are the things that need assessment and approval.
These are the things that need appropriate action.
The coming season is finding a way into his heart
and he plans for another summer of love and savagery.
Once again he will be spiritually reckless
and remove his soul's armour
letting her do with him
what any other season has done.

Only because anything is possible

The people who see him
outlined against anything courageous
believe in his fear of her.
He mentions her in poems about Berlin,
about meeting her in Paris
(possibly at the turn of the century
when she would have conspired
with artists and architects).
His love for her makes him restless
and though lesser men call him mercenary
his thighs ache for her
when he brushes past cathedrals
and other legends.
Still, he imagines himself shipwrecked
(possibly on the Grey Islands ...).

Never seeing Berlin or Paris,
her name, barely audible,
settles between rocks and gull bone.

Her birthday, July 25, 1985

He has waited twenty-one years to love her,
and though she is in another's arms
the agony is holier than before.
He watches her in public places
and sympathizes with others
in their pedestrian longing.
She is too brilliant to stare at,
so, blindly, he moves toward her,
her beauty dangerously perfect.

Yet there is no flower he would apologize to,
and no sunrise inadequate,
for everything must compete with her
and find its own place in line.

Listen to this, he tells the architects of love,
long after the angels have forgotten their favourite prayer
and stopped criticizing Jesus bravely for keeping them apart,
he will be the first to wash his lips with rain.

Sunday, March 9, 1986

The poet records a cold but sunny day
as he moves through another afternoon.

So tell Gower Street to tell St. John's,
the poet is refusing all bribes;
love's eventual splintered gallows
are not a sufficient deterrent.
While her eyes are still seen
through the city's haze
he will be singing.

la la lah lah la la lah ...

Don't be frightened,
the only light is the fire.
It was meant to flicker …
it is not to be shared,
not yet.

This mist does not cover every street
this sleep is never permanent.
Wait for daybreak, the brightness will
make this beauty less obvious.

Royal York Hotel, Toronto, Rm. 12–121, June 26, 1984

There was nothing in his heart
any less familiar than it was earlier.
She was torn between the Royal Ontario Museum
and the taverns of Toronto,
her anxiety transported from Nova Scotia.

The white heat made him nervous
and he remembered his condition.
"I am in love only seasonally," he said.
"I will be a martyr for my kind
if you will hold me once more."

Just when he knew he could love her
he placed himself on a 12th floor window ledge.
It was then he knew what he was made of;
he was to be spread evenly over the city.

He counted moments like seconds.
He laid them on his head with strategy
(in place of a holier, more pretentious symbol).
She took his outstretched hand and joined him.

There they stood, naked, a poet and a book-store manager.
When they jumped they both knew,
this is the way to be in love,
this is the way to sell books.

Mary

He's a stranger to those he admires.
Too drunk to say good-bye,
he only remembers her name.

Mary would have been his choice
if only she were willing
to accept this baptism
and be called anything but his.

1.

A weariness comes from loving,
neither fatigue nor muscular ache,
but deeper, much deeper, in the dream
near the centre, where nothing moves
and there is no light to reveal
the things that have been said.

A weariness comes from loving,
like something that has
refused to die,
longing to be let loose,
to tear apart the things that hide,
that are almost hidden,
deep, near the centre.

2.

Only when the harbour is calm
are they free to walk among the others,
where love is too vague to remember
and death to personal to discuss.

Department of Mines, 3rd Floor, Central Trust Building

He has just counted twenty-one cars
and decides it's a good time to stop.
Each vehicle has one or more occupants
who make their way along Bonaventure Avenue
to unheralded points in the city.
A siren gets his attention. Twenty-two.
This is what he does now,
they've hired him to tabulate movement
while waiting for her to come home.
Twenty-three, twenty-four, twenty-five ....

She was out, he was home

1.

He asked her ... were your feet cold
on Water Street last night.
If he could warm your mouth
why not your feet, as I would have done,
held them until the flattery of youth
was once more mine to give,
held them until this cold winter was in my hands
and he would see in us
what he sees in those birds
that ignore him from the rooftop ....

2.

He continues to arrange beads of sweat
and numbers them by colour.
They swirl around her forehead
only to move closer to her appetite.
He is somewhere between
what has been decided
and what is to come.
His hand has moved to her too often.

1.

He looks for her in small cafés,
the ones that cosmopolitanize St. John's.
He usually finds her there,
surrounded by salads and skateboards,
salads for maturity,
skateboards, maybe her preference.
Throughout all this he is without protest.
He pretends she wants him holy.

2.

He was found in St. Patrick's church.
All he wanted was to bathe on the altar
and smell Jesus' skin burn like his own.
He wanted to hold the body of Christ
and say to family and friends,
be happy and pray for me.
I am somewhere between love and mythology,
what better place to risk your life.

He's never seen her
take the hair from her eyes
and place it behind her ear;
that slow movement
that makes men run
from their reason.

It's the mornings he misses her most,
when he's not sure which thigh
deserves more attention.

The crisp sunlight is moving him
past the shadowed corners of winter evenings.
It is March 3rd, the following morning,
twelve hours since he has seen her.
He has said good-day to seven reluctant strangers
who seem suspicious of his attitude.
He waits for the trembling to stop.
He has to concentrate and work,
but in the face of certain disaster
his heart is free of heaviness,
her eyes have met his and once again
there is a new holiness ...
a new beginning for night and day.

Skies on top of crows, crows on top of skies

Whoever would have guessed,
on a day so wind swept,
that he would be
for those strangers' ears,
a drunken voice for their common fears.

A short letter, April 23, 1989

How many drinks has it taken
him to begin this short letter?
His cigarettes refuse to stay lit.
Outside, the moaning and pleading
of the Cape Spear foghorn.
It's still winter here, and on this
cold and wicked night she stands
on Signal Hill, admiring herself
silhouetted against the lights of St. John's.
She is cold but won't confess,
she is afraid but won't confess,
she is suffering but won't confess.

The man across the street
has just finished shovelling his steps.
He has now taken a broom
and begun to sweep away the clumped powder
to ensure safe footing for all
who enter his private life.
He seems pleased, and stands back
to marvel at the texture of the world.

This observer also marvels
at the texture of things;
the ordered chaos of his lover's hair,
the resilience of her ambitious arms.
His memory of her covers his routine like snow.
He does not want that man
with the broom near him,
for he too is pleased,
and wants a safe footing
for all who pass his own boundaries.

He is not calculated enough
to embrace the rules of the world
and lounge in its merciless rewards,
but he is ready to kill anyone
who accuses him of not loving her
while carving out a place for his soul
in the mountainous womb.

Monica, March 27, 1985

Two years ago today,
in a room of tile and stainless steel,
she reached out to the world
and with half-shut eyes
asked it to be lenient.
Her journey was beautifully gentle;
from the bathed comfort of one life
to the clamouring and reckless other,
she asked only to be loved.
    Two years later,
    with these requests secured,
    she bounds and squeals
    content with the order of things.
    And through her blossoming birthday eyes
    now seems to whisper
    to the man who has left her,
    I'm okay, I know who you are.

A poem Georgia O'Keeffe would have recognized her in

Now that he can embrace
the maturity of trees
and take some comfort
in the beauty of things,
her insistence
that people are worthy
will perhaps keep him from changing
what is so delicately meant to be.

So he takes the green fragmented leaf
and engraves her name on his wrist,
the insects hum their praise
amid the rage of the wounded forest.

He could have stayed,
her burning mood was unequalled
and his reasons for loving her
seemed equally unmatched.
He turned from the fractured window
and thought,
Oh Jesus, I want her more.

The morning ashes gave way to singing
and every living thing supported them.
Let's watch them, the living things said,
let's see if they lie to each other.
Lip on lip, moment on moment.

He covered his face to protect himself.
The woman who sat beside him, the woman he loved,
was throwing anything that would cut him.
Something struck his heart and he fell to his knees.
As he lost consciousness he dreamed:
    Who sings to her, who could want her more.
    Years were being pressed into cut roses
    just to let her have sunsets in her room.
    He was controlling the world for her,
    blue swirls of snow were being rerouted
    so as not to chill her past, present and future.
    He was even making arrangements to take the pain
    from her father's liquid life.
He woke to this:
Dry throat, darkness, blinding storms, frozen body,
bleeding heart.

Somewhere on the Newfoundland coast

Somewhere out in the desert
he was crawling to Minneapolis,
his cracked tongue scraping
along the fine mountainous sand.

They were almost lovers.
He should have talked more
and let her know how he felt
about Newfoundland and nationalism
but he couldn't get past her concern
for oil and fish stocks,
when all they had to do
was touch each other,
not the whole fucking country.

But now that he knows what the whispering is about
he has left St. John's in a rubber raft,
bobbing stupidly across the Atlantic
where the memories of the night sea have no colour.

There are places outside the city,
where in some bewildered mood,
he will take her well-ordered beauty
and show the yellow hay
what it must compete with,
and while kissing the anguine boundaries of trees
remove the summer's moisture from her lips.

Later, when the sun has placed itself perfectly,
they will move among the few remaining conversations
that can satisfy their hungry apprenticeship.

And, when the moon is running restless,
their love, and the noise of Water Street's remaining heroes,
will blend comfortably with the intimate echoes
of four hundred years.

So now he turns,
his back to the generous lover,
his thighs arched toward his death.
On some western shore
generations have misplaced themselves
leaving her to examine the ruins
of one man's pilgrimage
where he knelt
to raise his voice and pray.

So now he turns,
his back to the magnificent lupin,
his thighs arched toward his lover
where there are no horsemen,
there is only embrace.

They would have memories like that,
something like stills from old films.
The closest thing now
was dreamy CBC music,
but that was enough to push him back
to European cafés and museums
where they had been together and amused,
growing young in each other's arms.

She blew bubbles and he thought,
that is the way we will be,
that is the way the world will remember us.

At that moment, there was the room,
the memory and himself.
He was hoping his children
would hear him cry out
above the hum of their gregarious lives.
  Trees moved and moaned in a way so purposeful,
  it made him envious of spring's talents
  and he pleaded with winter to freeze the world,
  giving him time to adjust and prepare himself.
  Dotted grey-blue March skies sin shamelessly,
  ignoring all responsibilities for this man's labour.
  But tonight, the nocturnal lights glow protectively
  in his children's hearts.

She wanted more air in the room,
her heart was being crushed.
He wanted more love,
his flesh was being discoloured.
When the window opened, all of St. John's
ached itself in between them,
it was all so familiar.
She wrote her story in a diary,
he looked for fresh cement
and cast her name in urban stone.

That she might someday trip on her own syllable
and fall back in his arms
was all he could hope for.

Some are
like spring birds,
loud and easily excited.
Others are quiet and strong,
careful not to disturb
the cracks in the air.
Those that are left and ignored
are at the edge of the earth
where there are no voices.
For them, things
remain the same,
old friends become good friends,
there are no new friends ...
no trains leave the station.

What could he have given her
in place of his longing?
They could have stayed on the lettered doorstep
and whistled at the blue moon
until one of them tired of the melody.

What love costs him (approximately)

Once more he retreats to the
sanctuary that is his room.
The familiar smells, his brother's gift
of unfocused pool balls, the assorted music,
all show signs of support.
He is ready to stay in.
He feels he should read more
but is wary of the methodical pain,
the clinical path.
Knowing how love becomes history
before it becomes legend,
he chooses instead to try it again.
Placing fresh clothes around him,
scented soap and optimism
to accompany his physical and spiritual thirst,
he whistles and pushes through
the ragged edges of another night.
He is on his way to another
sixty or seventy dollar poem,
where the price per image
is not decided by the Canada Council,
but by the tolerance of friends.

This is to take with you.
He told her this
and it warmed her.
It was to ease things
and make the public
less aware of her,
make her wanderings
less erratic.
Be careful creating
on buses and boats.
He told her this
and she smiled.
She knew this distance
would be less painful
and she let the moment touch her.
The wind brushed her
in Cuckold's Cove
but ignored the berry pickers.
He loved the wind for that
and moaned for Jesus
to let them love.
In Middle Cove and River Bourgeois
the animals will be whispering.
They will whisper,
it is too dangerous, too perfect,
let nothing disturb them.

Friday, March 4, 1983, Holiday Inn, Gander, Room 136

To begin with
he thought of himself as spiritual,
principled if you like.
He would explain his aching loins
as something he was learning to live with.
Refusing the offers of love
and entertaining celibacy
he ignored what had created him,
what had made him a legend,
and walked into the arms of Jesus
without hesitation or shame.
Soon, Jesus in his wisdom
tired of him and his constant pain,
threatened his family with eternal sorrow
and then beat him on the pitiless steps of worship,
in front of every memory he had ever held,
in front of the only moments he had ever considered holy.

He was only vaguely aware of the card game.
His head reeled and bounced around her beauty.
Twenty-five someone shouted, and things focused.
Only then would he remove his heart from hers.
He would press his leg to hers, feel its warmth
touch the others in their traditional corruption.
Love was coming at him hard and fast
and it scared him. Will it be right this time,
will I be healthy he thought.
Two days later he begins to prepare himself. He prays.
Dear Jesus, please bring her home.
Let her know she has left me
smiling at the enemy. Let her need me
as much as you do her, for only
through her will your talent be seen
and your own sins be forgiven.

These are the times
for the whiskeyed pleasures of youth
when the world would prefer
loving Wednesdays
and that the marriage of summer
wasn't as loud
as the sentence of age.
All night on the water
not knowing whose feet he should kiss,
whose arms to claim,
he clings to the very words
that make the wounded free.
And there, where the trees
parted and slept,
where men stopped and complained,
two lovers kissed each other
and wished themselves
empty of spring.

Not knowing who to ask
he stopped a street-wise sparrow
and pleaded for direction to her heart.
A maze of flight forced him
to study footprints in the frozen snow.
To distinguish hers from the insignificant markings of others
was his unwavering purpose;
to chisel one from the reluctant landscape
and wear it tightly around his neck
until summer would remove the season's damage.

For the man who walks through the ruins of love
and wraps his feet in the bandages of battle

The man behind this brief justice
is unsure of himself.
The unfamiliarity of wind and tide
leaves him anxious;
he must shelter his mood
and perfect what some call his sentence.
He has no real illness
and no reason for ignoring
the apostles of verse.

Yes, it is I who fear Jerusalem
and the ecclesiastical frames of poetry
yet long to hear
the final words of decency
that tumble from the lips of saints.

Epilogue

Now that there are no cobblestones
and few old photographs
we are free at last,
we owe nothing to anyone.
The indigenous race,
we are responsible,
it was our choice.
Now that we have kept down
the souls of garrison soldiers
and with dirt and stone
moved the Beothuck once more
we can embrace this century,
and those to come ...
once more, as in 900 or there about,
looking into the hazy July morning
there will be bona vista,
no obstruction of guilt and memory.
But cry no more for the leaf
that swirls in the wake of panic,
the young man who drowned
in the harbour of North America's oldest city.
It is as it seems.

Revisions made on Newfoundland's 40th Anniversary of
Confederation with the Dominion of Canada, March 31, 1989

Oui, he knows them,
they are a mirror of his people
whose suffering is well documented,
not only in regional inequality
but in political shepherding.
Voices from the Betts Cove copper mines
have echoed in gunshot through
the American Civil War.
Later, this was paid for in occupation;
pregnant women carrying broken lives
for the future of the Western world,
free trade for free labour.

Do they sing in Gaspé?
They've stopped here;
only the slow moan
of a grinding submission
while loving thee smiling land.